# Against the Flight of Spring

*To Dennison
with love
and admiration*

# Against the Flight of Spring

*Allan Briesmaster*

Allan Briesmaster

QUATTRO BOOKS

The publication of *Against the Flight of Spring* has been
generously supported by the Canada Council for the Arts and
the Ontario Arts Council.

 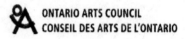

Author's photograph: Holly Briesmaster
Cover painting: Bert Weir
Cover design: Sarah Beaudin
Typography: Grey Wolf Typography

Library and Archives Canada Cataloguing in Publication

Briesmaster, Allan
    Against the flight of spring / Allan Briesmaster.

Poems.
Issued also in an electronic format.
ISBN 978-1-927443-38-5

    I. Title.

PS8553.R459A73 2013      C811'.54      C2013-900378-9

Published by Quattro Books Inc.
382 College Street
Toronto, Ontario, M5T 1S8
www.quattrobooks.ca

Printed in Canada

*for Holly*

# Contents

# IDENTITIES

## Identity

ONCE I WAS THAT, BUT NOW I AM THIS.
BUT WAS THAT ONCE I? AM I NOW THIS?
ONCE THAT, NOW THIS.  BUT – I AM.
*WAS* THAT  THIS?  AM  I  I?
I AM THAT I!  (THIS ONCE.)

## Grandparents

I never wondered aloud, nor was told in their house,
much about cranky Grampy – stooped, frail, thin, bald –
or, twice his girth, gentle Grammy, the plainest old woman
I'd seen, with her welcoming magnetic smile.

Dense-grey German accents with simplistic word-stores
left them quite childlike to me, and made quainter
the salt-thrower superstitions that strained my mom's patience;
though mostly they both drew a reverence I fully shared.

His well-worn carpentry tools rasped fragrant wood shavings.
He'd fix anything. She cooked roasts, mashed potatoes, peas,
beets, and thick-crusted pies. Beans and carrots were tended out back,
in front red roses. Indoors, velvet African violets. A lilac
stood at the side toward the engine plant's large parking lot.

*

Summers, he'd pluck the metal beetles off the roses,
drop them in oil. She laundered, crocheted and sewed.
Groucho would make him laugh. Sometimes I heard whispers
of his daily pass through Luther's Bible's block script.
Grammy prayed silently. Often just cleaned and scrubbed.

Twice Grampy rowed me around Broadbrook pond after sunfish
and pumpkinseed; spoke little, shared sweet butterscotch.
Mom once said he was palace guard to the Tsarina,
chosen for height; fled ahead of the Japanese war
to toil on the Panama Canal. Yellow Fever. Then coalmine.

Disinherited too, she came for new life in New York.
Began as a maid to a generous rich Jewish lady.
Sang a lot when still young, mom recalled. "Lovely voice."
Raised four kids, worked in the plant when it made rugs.
In her big-flowered dress, Grammy always gave me the best hugs.

## Child of Self

"I am my own child," the great poet said in his pride.
And what, and whose child, if any, ever, am I?

"I am my own man," I could say. "Unbeholden. The Chief."
(Maybe give myself a slight raise now, and extra time off!)

I was, am, the boy of my father, genetics affirms,
though more of my mother, in complex emotional terms.

In Dad's near-absence I struggled to clear my own slate:
in body, mind, heart, securing a private estate.

As if there were any choice in this entire matter.
As if some centre could cohere, not divide and not scatter.

Nor could I locate a mentor or real role model.
Gained a crude patience, muddling thru fast working-years.

Avoided much, withheld the thoughts that I made mine alone.
Or so it seemed. Observed, listened, got over small fears.

Waiting for what – a greengold gate to spring on its own?
Leaving the debt to the infant-within in arrears. . .

Today I'm a father and double as both parents too,
with dwindling time for bridging old rifts before I go.

To pull that off, in full, I'd best solve my sole self first.
I carry this fraternal twin in me, past-due its birth.

## Schema

**1.**
Too often falling short, so prone to shame –
did it all stem from willful temperament,
or genes entwined by fateful accident;
or are there further factors one can blame,
whose characteristics, passed ancestrally,
roll negative dice which, while they stunt and lame,
exonerate from culpability?

**2.**
Persistent drives into dissatisfaction
have never let fault-lines alone define me,
despite thin yields and general lack of traction.
Even self-consciousness can't realign me.
Nor am I ruled by action-and-reaction.
I step aside, some moments, to reflect...
forging forth most when not forced to *perfect*.

**3.**
This could become quite a humdrum conundrum.
The concept of "free will" was overrated,
along with what's been termed "determinism:"
what undergrads once earnestly debated.
I thought I'd bypass dualistic schism,
see multiple perspectives generated,
embrace the spectral and ancestral prism.

**4.**
Concerning all the ones who globally shaped me,
I choose to dwell on the essential good
(though recognitions have often escaped me),
giving due credit to the attitude
and the intent of gesture and of word
at dawning birth, more than tipped latitude:
the stance time cannot test. Which has withstood.

## Childhood and Now

Does childhood end? So many years gone by
without solidifying to the certain shape
adults revealed or put across to me. . .

Was there, along the line, a chronic failure
to conceive any self who could flesh out
destiny's limit?
                No, no way! – Although
I long outgrew my ballglove, even so
the pocket stays imprinted on my palm.

Not all the daydreams and fresh forms of play
get pounded from their skins, leaving dry leather.
A toughened nerve can still retrieve a touch.

Some nights I feel sharply as when I first looked up
to call and name the white-hot torch of Venus
or tall-shouldered Orion's belted sword.

## What Stayed Since

From far-northwest of now, the wild greenness
bears, upon you, a gaze you can't hold.

Once, in such fields among the clad mountains
you felt most alive. Compassing. . .what?

Only a strong dream portals you back there –
though nearly all names have since dissolved

with rain and mist. The first paths went long-lost
or lapse at clifftops where you had strode

beyond strange wind-trembled cottongrass, once,
. . .tussocks, lush lupine or high spire-weed,

then wound away toward a wide curving sweep
of black-sand shore and thunderous foam.

There, where big logs, bits of net, shell pieces
and fossils-in-stone lay spread and thrown. . .

What is this low light that drowns, that casts less
than memory for salvage of who

you were, those days, against pummeling seas?

And the far-green stares on, wildly, through

## Late Tongue

Walls planted inside, with reverence and fear,
banned me from kisses, deferred my chafing life
while others flexed and flared in their sunlight
winged with the strong imminence of embrace.

They knew just what to flaunt at my solitude,
how to exceed a slow uptake like mine.
Earth was not strange in such adept eyesight
already bent on long voyage or high flight.

When I broke from my grove, the sun's head was bowed.
Shadows touched, near the reach to the full river.
It proved more turbulent, less pure than I'd thought;
offered a luster far truer than a mirror.

Now I trace the vein that makes, ever stranger,
the loop from my sky's tongue, the surge through the sea.

## Schooled

You've lived enough to reflect how little
you learned, and what little. Songbirds have more
to teach, and dragonflies' conjugations,
and transitive verbs on the wind.

Filled with sluggish water, a small well
instead of a ruffling lake, you'd settle
for a fresh pond now, provided its air
were willow-shored and it fed a blue heron.

Sap in a March tree or the moist flame-colours
behind the green before it dries away. . .
To be their connective. Like encoded seed.
But nothing, nothing known before gestation

and birth in light, and not ever the dust,
down-layered and blown, that's left after.
Only the ongoing twist given your circle,
the sphere-shape inside-outed. That fruit.

That sole possibility, stretched-at to make
the implausible, leapt gap far-gone
beyond the sunshine's removal, become
undescended descendant, invisibly visaged.

Well-schooled in nothing, then: one booked
long since to turn and be turning, be tumbling
under and over the edges and tips
of the breaths of the leaves of some leaves.

## In Lieu of Reunion

I wonder, sometimes, how it goes with you.

And have you ever wondered how my land may lie?

Owning no house but a broad balcony
that steals the northeast light from trees and sky. . .

Sometimes hawks turn there, without thoughts or fears,
and scatter lingering shadows of ambition.

Despite derailment from my early mission,
I've known well-grounded love some forty years.

Would you believe I made beautiful friends,
finer than rainbow gold? – Though none like you.

With such deeply embedded navigation,
some of your loftier dreams must now be true.

Back then, what promise-full, fast orientation!

May more than wealth and power see you through.

## Workstream

I drew on sweat and flame. But they, untrained,
could not co-operate, and live, nor be

split out of me. So I contained
both, with a superficial parity:

on crest, down trough stretched and restrained,
daily absorbing routine shock
of hot pressed ice, emitting frigid steam.

I denied nightmare, waved off canyoned rock
without desiring what might have been gained
as monolith. Refrained. Disdained

to melt, crack, undermine, or ever block
this waking and unbreaking dream.

## The Belated Freelancer

Scraps of odd dream disperse on emerging
from when you were formless and young.
But whether the sun shreds their prospects
or some dire threat melts quickly away,
you no longer rise with inadequate shine
at the regathered nightmares of day.

Now you need not put on pervious armour
and haul yourself toward the jaws
of unbalanced bouts. For this fresh regime,
thick skin's nonessential, the nerves de-fray
from chafe and jostle, hard deadline, delay
and leaden routine. In morning's mirror

you see your own boss's scowl only.
Not impinged on by anyone else's
aggressive posture, dull nagging demand.
No boardroom edict, efficiency clinic,
no obtuse policy guideline to toe.
You've ditched both "on call" and compulsory flow.

The channels are clear, the leads open into
the once deferred farther shore. Found anew:
with know-how, un-mothballed, reanimated,
that won't ever cramp nor strain. Or, are you too
far-gone for shaking the one other day-mare:
of time lost. Of irreversible drain.

## Inimical

That jarring tone's amphibious innuendo –
stagnant in part, part stranded; all at sea.

Irritant – yet stealthy border-crosser
who drains goodwill and osmoses unease.

Foundational sand or littered nettled quagmire
breathing a sour fog fetid with loose rumour.

Blocker, distracter, dragger, tempting me
to lash at, or unwarily ape, such ways.

Not even a salving antidote of humour.

My long obsession – merely your latest craze.

## The Friends

Eye to eye, ear to ear; twinned open volumes.
Mere circumstance, the split durations' seam.

The in-depth content pours upward, exhaustless,
of a shared world, this overlayering dream:

galactic milk above, clear fount far-under,
well loving, but unbound by, planar clay.

Time-travelers, cut below the spun horizon,
they pulse light, with care, in their aerial play.

## The Partner

This life tears on, through progress and decay.
Past lives lie killed, while in the frantic present
one fades fast unless joltingly renascent.

It seems I'm frankensteined by innovation
that flattens futures into instants gone
and fouls the fields loved under antique dawn.

If not for *your* long constant new creation,
my spirit would be void of scope for play.
I'd lurch in shrouding whirlwinds of dismay.

You fortify a space to temper rages,
outmode regret, by timely consummation,
and charge me with a use for troubled age.

# Compass

*homage to Sonnet 116*

I'll only smooth the path for the wise pair
who love each other wholly as they are
and as they will be: never in despair
at wounds of change, hostile desire, or fear.

Those ones have powers that, through droughts and floods,
guide them more soundly than a satellite
beams GPS across the longitudes.

Free radicals and the earth's weight will fright
the slack skin crinkling over bending bones,
as titled waves of days accelerate;

but stronger care won't bow to such unknowns.
It shines with courage and warm tolerance
despite what dizzy media dictate.

I learn this, making real my own romance.

# Demi-visionary

Because you switched off all your near devices,
and walked a short sweet way before this ground,

you're standing ripe to catch these aerial spices
and let the all-but-lost, for once, abound.

The nectar of green June after rough rain;
the evening light passed from tree-tips to cloud;

a sense of having outlasted old pain:
and that your gauze of words need not be shroud.

To spy what lies in deeper, higher waiting:
the cache unsealed by the instinctual stroll.

Not willed, but patiently primed toward un-gating.
For oriole's loosening flash off poplar bough,

another's forage overhead on willow:
the nearest to life's heart "life" will allow.

## Clarities

One night I saw my name written in cloud
but afterward kept questioning who I am.
My own script seemed like rows of aimless puffs
whose hollow thunder could portend no rain.

Some said, we need to trek into strange lands,
live lean, bear pain, and more than flirt with danger.
Converge on the adverse, clasp its hard hand.

Instead, seldom excursing from the nests
of harmless work and pleasure, I hung back
oblivious to the unknown deity
who speaks, at last, through terror of Her lack:

*Not knowledge nor experience; by faith find*
*the full and empty clarities that sign*
*the presence in the desert of our words.*

# DARKENING

## Valuation

I'm needing more earth in my head, more sky
at my heart, less noise between. – To hear what?

You skillful gamers and shiny victors,
is *that* the one-trick proof of our finished worth?

Down the historic rift, across inching rock,
swiftly before eclipse toward extinguishment,

everyone missing the goal line of goal-lessness
by an infinite hair.

## In Dissent

I must decline to buy into the hype
and smartass rationales greasing these movements.

Let me be left alone or left behind
the aggregate herd-minded lunging drift
that takes each disassociated psyche
without foresight toward ditch or pit or wall.

The tainting of the earth, ocean and sky
never gave pause for notice, much less thought.

When there's no edge derived by mild constraint,
and as fast wheels and oily credit roll,
who needs a fixed, maintainable abode
next to some salt gulch or slime-plugged canal?

The incense off this, rising to ex-heaven,
presumes a mega techno-miracle.

## Rhymes for End-tymes

In those bright times when graphics displaced wording
and drum-tracks pulsed the sampled tune-o-mation,
what had held spirit-fire became strobed smokescreen,
and stun and jolt outmoded revelation.

Tighter nerves wound around deeper narcoses.
The digital remastering of the past
preempted unassisted anamnesis,
while brains bored further into the scintillant blast.

Then if we waken to a worldwide quake-down,
wiped of skills, common sense, and common lore,
we'll dry like parasites that killed their hostess,
as our last consoles drain of juice and gore.

# In Torpor

Shadows congest now
on empty swamp:
tortuous, moonless,
inert in absence
of the water flocks.

Who were you, sunken
relic, amphibian
lost from what flew
naked plumage once
into skies far away?

# A Form of a Cry

What quake will ever heave these compact cinders,
what shudder cleave their solid groan, and shear
this mesa piled and shelved with tabulation,
abandoned unexpired remorse, curse, fear –

Where are the scarlike lips, how tear them open
for other than a mumble or a moan?
How could the heat revert out of such ashes,
so long after its coils of breath crushed down?

This pile's core bears the equal rage to wrench it,
crack light beyond the leaden rim, sky-bound,
break into space not crusted, never barren:
at once new base and lidless vent.

My sound.

# Trajectories

Lees of the sun do their nightly dissolve.
My little path, too, dries and dims.
    I'm scraping what's left aboveground,
    that could colour up dreams.

I starved this day's wish to out-glare
the pointblank of noon or at least upend
    the narrowing expectations
    in the eyes of my friends.

The cosmos roars on toward dispersal
in backdrop soup or sucking holes –
    as we ourselves have inflated
    the melee and sped the falls.

Still, though, on a quiet day I hear
surviving bees' earnest work
    to remake future roses: out
    from compost, against this quick dark.

# Nowhere Here

*"going where I have to go"* – *Theodore Roethke*

I have to go off-world. This little one
is overrun with noise and fume and speed.
It's undermined by fear. The clever greed
that drives the mighty to trademark the sun,

to hoard its warmth. A universal stun,
.if not pained lonely in addictive need;
bamboozled by the most simplistic creed.
Soft touches lost at every handhold won.

Off-world I go. Not giving up my being
in violent despair. Not on a tear
with some intoxicant. Not lamely fleeing

to rustic resort, retreat anywhere
ascetic or remote. The one flight freeing
from all such    is imagination's care.

## Dilemma and Remedy

1.
At each decimation of the early stars,
under the mists from cinders, I withdrew
through nebulous and vacant substitutes.

Tall oligarchs ruled then, by wealth and fear.
Competitive betrayals tilted things:
even the weather, paths ahead, the soil.

Sun became foe to sight. Moon hurt the brain.
And what, now, can elude such sour air,
chemistry that infiltrates the water.

False mirrors dried in cracks across this mouth.
I'd amputate myself from their engorgement,
but no clean blade is glimmering anywhere.

2.
Only my solar friend works the reversal.

He dreams a benign moon aloft whose tide
unclogs the estuary of reflection
with robust, cleansing nutriment whereby

I am disgorged. New channels down my veins
admit green breath that exhales greener nurture.
Wide lucid moods then sash the temperate earth:

letting reciprocal assists and gifts
flow bountiful, as from an opening hand.

## At Dusk

Profiles of things fade, the way words
will falter at less than a whisper:
and meaning loosens, to form
an alliance with silence.

The mundane bell vibrates a stillness
weighing on its own shadow. Between
held breaths, the ember-colours
tinge down, collapse, crumble off.

Perception flees after twilight.
Relic shapes lock interchangeably
in a collage of absences
across the blending field.

No frame, no verge. Diminishment finds
a terminus. Earth embodies air.
The light sinks to soil; thick dark
suffuses upward as mist.

Image, sequestered from message, rests
on the long oil which, under lids
of common solitude, feeds
the ignitions of sleep.

## Nocturne

For once, a calm wide open night
pierces with less-thin constellations,
like those before the rise of cities –
felt, not nostalgically, but by sheer
subsidence onto what was, and is.

In noiseless trance the grey veil withdraws
from nighthawk, below shooting star:
a cool salve spreads over broken slopes
and a breath blooms back among the names
of owl, and firefly, milky way

# BUCOLIC

## Stroll, Early March

Leaving my snug frail castle, I displace
its narrow rhythm with a winter wind's
not-too-late icy staccato ripple.

I scan the indents where old snow still hides
its long-refuted rind from solar reason

and taste, in the tasteless cleanliness of snowflakes,
the breathy land not wholly lost to change.

The graveyard and a few heritage homesteads
lie back as though their pasts could verily be;

and now, recalling my postponed vocation
on highroads toward the nevermore, I see

a spirit outside history's cannibal jawline
blow off the spread salt of faux certainty
and scatter outworn doubt's own cold white dust.

# Snowdrops,

lanterns of longer light
through the coarse final snow,
you stir up such pang-tinged thoughts
with your pure blank tips,

forerunning all the other ephemera,
from bud to curling petal,
in worm, beak and nest,
up across wispy cirrus: under

the rounded headlong domain
of that omnivore the sun
whose earth-tilted shout
dissolves, too, in air.

## Against the Flight of Spring

Oak tree and locust tree, slow to leaf,
prolong the Spring by a common reserve,
admitting sunshine through still-bare limbs
on accents of fragrant phlox, white anemone:

all to the chorus of the tiny, fierce,
dainty warbler, the loud brazen jay,
pert-whistled cardinal, loquacious wren;
each proclaiming their open terrain,

only to subside in fast-mounted heat,
darting less often through slenderer gaps
with underleaf-pale or rich-colour flickerings,
like scattered recollections of forgetting;

while just a few keep their retrograde outcry
apart from the rush to be earth's.

## Uncurtaining

*off Yonge St., Thornhill*

Swishes of so many tires on asphalt –
pervasive, though the brain largely damps that down.
But through every flank of dullness this evening
pierce whistles, the shrill-fluted and sharp-barred cries
inmixed with chippings of beak-like peck-like sounds

that draw this listener out to an elsewhere
ablated off the gridline, re-routing far
from that longest of streets... Here my balcony
looks toward the northeast, on unimpeded green
which intimates an alternative transport

whereby grey lanes back-channel and drop to naught.
Soon, greenly slow light reveals just how much this
branching shade differentiates. How it's blued,
warms with round yellow-glow, or keeps hints of pink
that redden up on each variable crown.

Then eyes that reach after flickering flights there
relinquish under the high shine of deep May
(every bough full-fledged) all kept, perspectival
focus and linear dominance, yielding
before the plebeian garden of the ear;

and the ear, loosed onto loftier sleep, here,
uncurtains for airs waved both distant and near,
and, by clear, sheer inner wind's counter-shielding,
upholds ramparts that let rare peace respire:
serene in the ambit of this vivid choir.

# From the Encirclement

June morning sunrise leaks in through the curtains
and dissolves the soft shadows on our walls.
The birds we love supplant the moon lost to us;
the velvet quiet bows to the spears of their calls.

Now bodies' rhythms ride the solar impulse,
the spiraling updrafts, their aerial grade,
though spirit fears the counterpull through down-spin:
subductive, under stealthily lengthening shade.

Soon the cool sun-lid winks out in the branchtop
where beaks of eventide dispense regrets,
and massive night-haze drowns within its dankness
the buoyant yearn for inconceivable states.

What will *transfix*, beyond all desperate reaches
toward strata that won't pierce yet can't encase?
We seek the look, the touch to bare and breach us
a dazzling dark no dawnlight will erase.

## In Changing Summer

Early July, full-stretch at the green zenith,
the large leaves of *no more* become bouquet
for insects. A cicada starts to saw
where sun balloons and almost retrogrades
along the hazed horizon's tilting centre.

An orgy of stuporous roses excresces
about as much or more as recollected:
with full impunity off swirl and spill
from its thorned nest along the arboretum.

Swallows dart their routine ecstasy,
goldfinches undulate in pairs or threes.
Assorted songbirds divebomb crows, and both
harry the lumbering hawk despite the hour.

Vital tall verdigris conceals, as always,
the patient calm of the wood skeleton,
while, beyond wish, copious grasses
(that must be mown sometime) run on.

The same! – But how, after what poured unchecked
so long from us, do we know anymore
if we will ever catch this same degree
of avian-sung verdure, once, again?

Never before this year through the short night
did the high heat of day subside so little.


*Thornhill, ON, 2010*

## Hearing the Grass

How we implant a voice on quiet things –
make the lawn say "I'm pleased at being trim
(but let me loose, I will escape your wish)."

Press an ear down, now, though, and dare listen
to sounds below a soft whisper's threshold.
Hear green whirr from whole choirs of chlorophyll,
notes held. . .
                    though your left ear fills in
with swaths of all-business-ridden clangor,
untuned to humbler anonymities
that sing outside the measures of our scores.

# The Spruce We Saw

*near Port Renfrew, Vancouver Island*

Evening was descending on the narrow road
that twisted with creeks under fir-covered slopes
and by breaks into stony, scrubby clearcuts.
The moss-hung boughs we passed along the banks
played half-familiar Island repetitions
of varying strangeness. Then on the local map
you saw the words "Giant Spruce," and so I
was set to stop when a small sign announced
"Harris Creek Spruce." A short path led in through
a grove of thinner trunks toward one dark girth.

It had begun to rain and you chose to stay
inside the car. You said only much later
you felt uncommon darkness radiating.
Not feeling any such thing, I approached.
A moss-streaked bole rose up, more broadly spread
than any I had seen – multi-flared base
like that of an old Soviet rocket, massed
as necessary to uplift the long ascension
of the black pillar's dozen-foot vast width,
stretched almost undiminishing, on and on,
until lost in great darkgreen upper branches.

Reaching, I touched the bole's cool soft surface.
Just seconds after, somewhere overhead,
a single crack of thunder detonated.

Then I felt, more inference than feeling:
*this is a being*; nothing of our day
sticks to it. Pillar darker into *black*
than that word or its idea could relate.
This entity that claims its own dimensions,
in midnight of a nonhuman awareness.
This tall simplicity, aloof from sun,
from civil knowledge, without the least link
to heart or hand. Lone, in-itself shrining,
hermetic, in full alien plenitude.
Utterly other.

– Though later you surprised me with the claim
you sensed a "vortex" (and then I no longer doubted
it was well you'd kept away). "Nothing
malign," you said; slow swirl of primal power.

And once I'd safely driven off, you told me
that you had looked back: and saw, high-up,
two prongs, or horns, protruding from the crown.

## From Lakeside Sand

*for H.*


Paused on another of the sometime coasts
along this inland sea, in lowering sun,
we can retreat, together here alone,
to eye the tumbled waves' loose placid thrusts.

In a foreshortened bay, two piercing-bright
gold bands float firm atop its lobe's blue darks;
and, in between, a bobbing flock of sparks –
flotilla, metallic and jeweled – burns into light.

These fleet, unearthly scintillations ensoul,
with added beams from our own fires onshore,
a mortal yet full-vital metaphor
that underpins one gaping, boundless whole.



*Cobourg, ON*

## The shining sun

is also one
explosion, held in hand, we know,
by mighty gravity, except
for out-burst heat    and all the light
amongst the invisible blasts
whose deadliness our air
blocks partly by
its blue sheet and white blanket.

Floating flower-centre
(found at eclipse to be)
corolla-petaled,    this our human star,
so roundly steady motioner,    severest
portioner of life-enough,
amassing    the spun furious rage
to act and be    supreme
rondure and highest hearth for us,
engine of weathers. . .

Hard global eye, unmeetable
source-logo for authority,
model and monopole for faith,
for judgment, endless rule
over the earth by cosmic law;
lone column of irrefutable surety,
progenitor of daily mundane awe –
small wonder she
was goddess, once, or god.

# Fungi near Lost Lake

Down the path into the woods, through subsiding showers,
the band of friends makes its way toward Lost Lake.
Sunbreaks flashing between clouds, with liquid sparks,
enrich the red/gold leaves flamed overhead
and glistening underfoot. . .when we start seeing,

half-buried in leaf-fall, shelved and enclustered
toadstool, lush honey-leather, puff, comb-coral.
Cap, crust, ruff, button, cone, or garish dotted slime.
The transient genitalia of the undersoil,
whose non-mortal offspring thrive in unknown dark.

Those pale micelial threads, extruding and probing,
are not just rootlets, mouth-parts, gut-tracts alone.
Interlaced all-around, through indefinite wide yards,
their species possess and rule all the nether-woods.
Far more than conduits drunk with existence, they

are at-work intellects. Intent neural nets
spread useful data about. Multifarious
minders, tenacious laboratories, they test
the composition of bordering compost,
send scouts of themselves on open-ended quests.

They relegate relic forms into formlessness,
break toxins down, neutralizing their threat,
transform what's moribund into the stuff
of relentless vitality under the carpet
of death. Are symbiotes, too, with the upright trees.

We tramp aboveground in alien ignorance
of labyrinthine tubules aloof from our air,
remote from sense and thought's grasp almost utterly:
well-buried, much like the links back to our innards,
behind the lighthoused coastlines of our brains.

*Their* infra-spreads become the capillaries
for gross benevolence. As if – so it would seem –
their reality were primally non-malefic.
As if the whole below-ness for which they are proxy
outmassed the sunned Manicheanism of things.

Could, then, one of our longest-unmet longings
be to re-root and re-merge in the dark of earth,
becoming threaded somehow through that substrate,
de-centred there, in amorphous bliss? What new fruit
might mount, for a good while, from the source below?

*

Now the companions emerge from half-shadow
onto the stone lip, to stare through lifting mist
at arrayed warm trees across a grey water's
undulant quavers and small intersecting waves.
Water: long-circular in-constant fundament. . .

Soon that sought lake, and the remembrance of seeking,
will leave a porous moist loam upon dispersion:
its melt of lonesomeness, of walls of the strange.
So it's not foliant light we will take with us,
off the nether of unspoken bond and mesh,

but a strong friendly embrace, tended onward,
through the broad networks from which each of us came –
outside the powers that pile plastic and steel;
in the rich soil of persistent affection,
living less for *what I want*, than by *how we feel*.

## a snowfall

air has transported
its new-borne weight
onto twig and bough

*

cold-aligned molecules
bristle there; disregard
how they were water

*

look aside, walk away
from metal murmur.
now taste the white-dark

*

in, through a floated gap
almost of silence – tickings.
(those crystal tines)

*

long thoughts bedded-down
under halfway sleep
draw toward the lost

*

turning back, you bear
core warmth, still, across
this one pale layer

*UT PICTURA*

## O pen

loosen the silence
give my tongue words
gift my words' tongue

rhythm this pulse
pulsate this rhythm
split the blank space

fuse the dank split
fire its dark
darken its fire

yield a long water
water the yield
flower this dust

flower the long dust
with such pollen
open o pen open

## Quasi-Dedalian

Gone from a cloudy world to a dry,
they got the straight view, without the rain.

Was there no way to hover between?

*


To hover between, you need wild wings,
a stubborn doubling-up of vision,
and a sly knack for taking tumbles

that slip into fortuitous turns:

though these draw contempt and derision
or get ignored, the tighter the burn

## Advice

Sun is untouchable by grief

Life glides on, at odds with beings

Higher than mountaineer, lower than miner
but not so far as a star through the eye,

in between entities a wind roves

Hear the diaphanous chords it inflames –
and melody blossoms for all

## An Abstract Painting

It's there in the tensions, is it?
    the ways they flare,
averting decorous peace.

*Not* the straight "scene" the medium
    clears, with pretence
of accurate illusion;

not objects referenced, assigned
    tidy placement,
foreground, mid-range, on, far-back.

No facile exercise of skill
    at modeling
the lit and shaded volumes.

It's in the struggle, never all
    resolved: to play,
past colours' disposition,

that music which is feeling, scored
    (wondrous to say)
for every visioning ear.

Half-open tablet's un-barred notes
    whose tone new eyes
orchestrate without key;

impromptu script whose lightning cues
    your gaze can't miss
by allured, free conduction;

prompt of silence itself to scale
    irises and
illumine the tympanum

along resistance from an un-
    sure circuitry.
Untempered strung wirings,

that let the twang of stressors
    dis-articulate.
Lacunae, lapses, traces,

impeding both stasis and glide,
    crack pattern; form
crosscurrented conundrum.

Rough relics, too, of slip of hand,
    snag back, perverse,
on a beholder's lenses.

Not only shown there, though – still less
    in merest "craft,"
in finesse. But where rhythms

rumble on to large assembly
    frictioned by detail
yet echoed-over, even

as flows of merged, permeating
    maelstrom and tide
bear to or from edges through core. . .

Into dimension 4, or more,
    totality then
utters its quaking stillness.

The interstices, with vexed lines
    of final force
tangling Particle in Whole,

spume out, while under-towed across
    the gravid gape:

spanning the chasm they keep.

# Poetic

*Poetry everywhere is inseparable in its origins*
*from the singing voice and the measure of the dance.*
– Sapir

The body it sings from, and sings into,
must be manifold, be "protean" – of course;

and while surging to a subsonic measure,
must also move in ways that leap and skip.

A cavernous bass beat, below the veinstream,
companions wild melodic bubblings-up:

that whole span palpable as somehow-songcraft,
no tuneless numbness; and with stumbles banned,

it tangos on. And if it trail, or halt...
a quiet or tense gap    just adds a rhythm.

A freshening uncharted pulse, taking on shapes,
harmonic firehose tipped with an apt nozzle –

the spray from which wave-sparkles fierily,
much though the out-arc bend, eddy, and roil,

its flux or cascade glancing-off light, too,
of moon and zodiac, their fires high-ridden

onto brisk breath, that leads the footed air
and swishes the undulating syllables;

...though they forget sea-chasm, earthy magma
under floors where *this* dance, and this song, do not.

# Aesthetics 102

Can any thing, on its own, be inherently
beautiful? For instance, a slab
of cold mutton. What everyone who
isn't starved will regard
with revulsion.

Could the right context induce,
and clever lighting-design conjure,
even it to lend itself – the brown-
purple colour, wooden texture, tendon
and bone – to join in, say, a
pleasing tableau, split-off as if
by an ethical prism
from appetite?

Or, consider for instance
a *C.S.I.* corpse: beatified
through luminous framing, probed
and graphed, zoomed-into
(mysterious, plush
lurid riches put to good use).

　　　　. . .It's almost
as though cosmetic lenses,
cool implements and fast gadgets, plus
dry wits of semi-poetic justice
are in themselves the answer
to any secondary victim's
prayer.

## Pollockian

Out of the lengthy
brush becoming tongue for wrist

begetting and beguiling
wildness

innumerable swirls
that entangle
along the up-against, the thrown

nest of pulsing threads

arrhythmia energized,
thrust    onto a skein

flung intersections,
lashing-lines

thicket of tangled dream

crazed outburst and thick spasm
preserve    in scar
on scar

stains, leaks and oiled wires
curlicue

to nowhere else

volume    of raving silences

still literal, the
inextricable
drip on scrape; soak, flick

and severed (s)pillage

un-containment
one    framed mounted
cosmos, hung

anarchic and centripetal

continuous dis-
continuum

unbinding   bound

## Rothko Notes

*i.*

negative cloud
in band on band

pillow-soft, a spectral
girder      triad
dimming, looming,

part
the lips of themselves for
proffered immensities


stacked high horizons,
    tender-fraught suspension
in wan-weighted shade

flat saturation, layery
    or intermelting
veils     of fade


deep shadow-bruise unhealed
on stain     scrape and scrub

    to half erasure:
blushes gone dark-pale


    skinned set plates re-
serve introverted shine

soaked masses
            levitative
    between rise and decline

    forceless fields     inroll
among withdrawals

*ii.*

hummed moods hold in mid-
swing (brune over plum)

    tinted breaths
round-cornered ragged-topped

absented mirrors    hazing
back at the subjectless
    part-stopped


far-advanced recessions in-
to, away from, and out
    of blankest pallor

vistas that spell dissonant
awe
through castaway colour

    ecstatic terror


*iii.*

abyssal lament    forlorn
    for world-loss past
    and/or oncoming

remote imminence
    of a vast, vatic mourn


persistences, absorbences'
    torn sunken bloom

pregnant ultra-sounding,
closures, fates, felt doom


    without finality

end after end

# In a Room of Milnes

*Art Gallery of Ontario*

How cold these are. And still. A dim
patina shrouds each one. And, from
inside the surfaces, there leaks
a shadowiness. Old shadings.

Drab, almost. A certain dullness creeps
into the very colours, even orange,
even red. Muted, scratchy. Scrape-like. Thin.
And yet a subtle lunar glow

comes on. A rooftop slants palely away
and back; dark swaths of evergreens
bristle, recede. Blank lakewater,
and a snow-covered meadow, float,

a hill rises in air. Some clouds
cloud. And re-cloud. Then transparence
of a simple glass jar gives out
plain white gleams at the lip and neck.

Mere tilt of a pole, shape of a shed,
a staid plank-sided house or cabin – how
their posed suggestions co-irrupt
forsaken spaces into presences,

and bring on a full emptying of time.
Resistance to oblivion. Between motion
and stasis. How thoroughly each
patch of texture gains a careful warmth

and infra-human tone. – Not comforting,
but still a rough assurance. Open. Broached.
How they each, then, do move. Move into us.
To stay: insistent. Stay. And stay.

# Of the Painted North

*McMichael Canadian Collection*

In between back-here and out-there the great forms convene:
angling wide, shifting, held slow among strokes of cold colours.

Up from the gravid dark, their long-range, marshaled contours
press against *no more*, toward *this is* and at *we have been*.

Sky, waters, cloud, rock, trees, by stormy alliance
with human touches, resist the inconsequent past.
They sign beyond stillness, in deft-handed gestures made fast:

non-animate yet alive across listening silence.

Soulless, ensouled. Deep-aloft, implicate on-below:
as, throughout bleak fleet watercourses of dispersion,
ripple far whispers, ingrown motions, calmer immersions –

their tough artifices. Heart-stone, bedded in that flow.

The unsettleable lands rise, which we dream we can know.
Tumult smoothes, wrested asway through the blue fluent snow.

## Lines Toward a Portrait of T.

Give round, strong harmony to the entire oval
under the pinned-back darkbrown-henna coif.
Carry that, soft, onto hillocks on cheekbones
and the faint parentheses around her mouth.

Rest a slim cupid's-bow across full lower lip.
Transfer sparkle from warmbrown eyes which, downturning,
show subtly blued lids beneath slender brows.
Now choose – the open glow, or pensive semi-close.

While she writes, make the chestnut-rim glasses perch
toward the lower nubbed width of proportioned nose.
Blend-in tones photographs might seek yet never speak:
of bemused endurer whose confidence only grows.

Indicate the fine neck. Hint a pearl earring.
Above demitasse chin, a halfmoon shadow-streak.
In all, show new grandmother as thriving young woman.
Place the beautymark, there, up the mid-left cheek.

# Harbourer

*after a collage/mixed media painting by Deborah Harris*

She stands in effigy of a guardianship
before the outward water: with close gaze
meant less to fend the necessary wind
than to deter prospective menaces.

So adamant a facial strength could stem
only from interwelding contradictions
onto dynamic steadiness, wreathed round
by those three dark thin sailing crescent scraps

haloing her stony glance as if they're twirled
above the headdress's back-bristled quills,
or spars of grey mist aura'd in a force field.
Explosive while impassive; held at will.

\*

As revelation leaks out through enigma –
emptying things inside toward things beyond,
transferring the beyond within – you ponder
what odd permuted layers the human takes,

how we push past the wholesomely "organic,"
propelled instead to cobble and erect.
So we will stitch our harbouring deities
with debris from the dreams of all we lacked.

## Mark Rothko's No. 2 – Three Tones

**1.**
Blue came on foremost when I first looked off at the ocean.
Such depth of colour, that clear day, with sheer immense mass
in that heighted body filling the entire horizon. . .
from where the Atlantic ran southward, ten thousand miles vast.

**2.**
We could say, this near-seven-foot canvas offers triple aspects.
Colour. Paint-stroke textures. A silent, spacious mood.
Showing how perfection itself, in Art, must lie imperfect.
How the truest fullness can not be full exactitude.

Look: the bottom blue rectangle can't help but evoke a sea-scene,
up through its dark-cobalt bulk's primally lower place;
above which, that shoreline-streak stretches across, yellowgreenly.
Atop it, the orange-glowed bar of dawn-lit open space.

The same-size, fainter band echoing that in a greenish-yellow
suggests a mirage of transparency onto beyond,
while what might convey yellow sky is edged ragged-and-hollow:
its rectangle dissolving, black, off along the high end.

But notice, all these bands and scratchy shapes float over absence;
a frame in plain black looks on each side to be eating back –
until and unless we revert to perceiving the colours
as "windows" – yet obviously they aren't really acting like that.

They exist as paint, cross-streaking into thin uncertainty,
by vexed intent, with a slapdashing half-saturation –
were this mere "design." But that hazy indefinacy
induces the eye to participate in a creation.

**3.**

Now I come to see back, past, yet farther-into the first ocean,
and a most recent one, the blue bay toward the headland dunes
near Valparaiso – as if just my eyes touched their gold.

Now, also, more blackness, the lower I look in *this* blue.
And I see the dark void or night ocean below all three tones –
yet the mirage-like band still prompts toward a visioning-through...

I grasp, in the abstract, as well, the idea of suggestion.
And I feel the roughness in existence, the drown into death.

Feel the improvised painterly messiness, turning transcendent.
And feel deeper waters go on, under skies of my earth.

## Ab Ex Redux*

a sign pointing
   to itself

the coloured cry
of violent

anxiety
   in torsion – as
enormous mouth

gesture of savage
reach
breaking from stillness

these and more
   build, manifold
without
      external prop

   so you
are monopole

*written at an exhibition of Abstract Expressionist paintings

# SOURCES AND SHORES

## Into Twilight

*after "Luz Ultima" by Juan Ramón Jiménez*

Late gleams, at play on the tips of the woodland crown –

quavering, you toss and scatter as though
the fallen sun cut you loose and has let you go.

Tumbled apart with the wind over dim branches,
what else is left for you now that the source is down?

Shimmer yourselves across to this blank leafage
hoisted against the encompassing grievous dark.

Transmute your gold through my pencil-slim near-reaches.

Together, let's leave a durable mark.

## After Evening Wine

I favour mild spring twilight, lounging
in the aftergleam of orange west
and misty-violet east, with glass
of Noir in hand warming and cooling.

The red tree-buds were dipped in cold flame
off that latest vintage of sunset:
all the plump shelljackets on them due
so very soon to pop and scatter.

Insistent indigo deepens now,
melting away into chilly black.
Not even enough left in my glass
to bathe that one thorned star's reflection.

Mellow but certain as night I'll rise
to face what pours through my desktop screen.

# Give praise

                bird-like, unto the given
blue of resounding blue silence over

shimmery goldleaf-gold as it flies
atop a lone yellow maple – riven

through the whole time we are ripped alive
from image on into memory    driven

to sing the gain in the sound that plies
the waking wind-swirl after we sever

by dint of a less frangible ash,
which won't shake loose from the score of its cries

(marrowed and feathered with fire)
until the reverse of forever

## Songbird,

        the sky you bring down so near,
unst(r)ained by any weight or dull soil,
confers transparence of heart that draws
immediate soul from springs below
your piccolo throat
               without a claim
to dominion – but yet a dweller
beyond the clutches of desire,
when all the call-notes plash and pierce-through.

We are flown free: a moment plum(b)ed, winged
in the ear of the one, only song.

# free-flight

*homage to José Acquelin*

you hear the bird as you do, thanks to your star
in moments when logic itself seems mirage
breaking the habit of dust

and all at once mobility needs no wing
and in this universe off its edges
the dark in your light lifts like fog

## Coastal Poem

*a response to "Poem" by Fernando Pessoa*

The blue light of a pacific quietude,
unbroken, in a singular steady wave
reared out beyond the shore-line of horizon

blues this near sea: on toward the wrinkling fingers
that ply the tuneless, measureless background roar
and hiss from overlap of foamy cymbals
brushed by pulses without channel or a name,

corroding all notation shelved on the sand.

*

If only there flowed in from such cold wonder
some base assurance, some rip-tide surmise
. . .that the whole dome and fluent depth below it
bond: as life itself might do, with that which is.

## *Nada* Revisited

*after Jiménez*

Against the naked evidence I tried
to mount the redoubt of an intellect:

secure, tall lookout from which I'd inspect
the coastline and the breakers and the tide.

If I skimmed light off that penumbral slide,
mustered a will more robust and direct,
summoned a voice no wind would intersect,

might my designs, merging at length, abide?

o

All seems for nothing. I could sink to nothing,
should shapes collapse I've conjured with my thought.

Yet every true creation stems from nothing.
It's out of voided chaos things get wrought.

Still, nothing built on nothing remains nothing –

as I, unless there's consciousness, am naught.

## Near-silence

When empathy dims and the conduit
to intuition
clouds

and fleeting slumber stays
moored at the quay

then if hard with dry glare your eyes
insist mine steer
for outbound skies

my recourse is at most
to free

these jetsam cries that ride
across the ear inside

tasting of soundless
unlettered sea.

## Outlet

*after "Loophole" by Pessoa*

In my bleakest frame of mind,
feeling filled with emptiness,
smog-enwrapped, walled in duress,
all promise pressed to rind –

if, then, I only straighten, lean
my head back, firmly spined,
look on the robust rise, or kind
withdrawal of the sun –

existence freshens with thought.
The colours may be a screen,
but prospects angle through; and out
a knothole's portal I come

unbound from wish, as from shame.
Trusting the brief given light.

## Bon Voyage

The earth's curve softens
        under wider sun
        Departing!
    A thump in the ribcage;
    shorebirds chime
    of brevity
Alternate outlets crack
    the corridor, to skies
    rainbow footed    or
        auroral
In feminine darkness
    this lit ship    casts off

# Notes and Thanks

Twelve of the poems in this book were in the chapbook *After Evening Wine* (Alfred Gustav Press, 2011). Others appeared in these anthologies and journals: *Decabration, Draft, Ropedancer, Saranac Review, Seek It: Writers and Artists Do Sleep, Spirit Eyes and Fireflies, Verse Afire,* and the online magazine *canadianpoetries.com.*

"Identity" was written in response to one of James Dewar's on-the-spot "themed poetry challenges" in the Hot-Sauced Words reading series in Toronto, as was the sonnet "Nowhere Here." (Thank you, James!)

The "Grandparents" are my maternal grandparents, in whose house in Broad Brook, Connecticut I lived at age 9-10. That poem and six others collected here were written at a workshop led by Barry Dempster in Chile in January, 2011. I am very thankful to Barry, to everyone in the workshop, and especially to Susan Siddeley, gifted writer and wonderful host, for the peak experience of those two weeks at Los Parronales.

"What Stayed Since" looks back to the time when, age 10-12, I was on Kodiak Island, Alaska.

"In Lieu of Reunion," the first six poems in "Bucolic," and the last one in that section, as well as the first two in "Sources and Shores," are all set at or near my home in Thornhill, Ontario. Lost Lake is in the Muskoka region, not far from Bracebridge, Ontario.

"*Ut Pictura*" is part of the famous phrase *ut pictura poesis* ("as is painting, so is poetry") from the Roman poet Horace's *Ars Poetica*. The ekphrastic poems "Pollockian," "Rothko Notes," and "Ab Ex Redux" were composed on-site at the exhibit of Abstract Expressionist paintings from New York's Museum of

Modern Art which was at the Art Gallery of Ontario in the summer of 2011. When I wrote "An Abstract Painting" (at an earlier time), I did not have any particular painting in mind.

Besides the source-poems and poets acknowledged under some of the titles, I gratefully credit the following poems, encountered in translation, for inciting me to attempt to emulate them:
"Late Tongue" – "Life," by Vicente Aleixandre
"After Evening Wine" – "Morning Coffee," by Gyorgy Petri
"Give praise" – "How the Bird Singing," by Juan Ramón
    Jiménez
"Near-silence" – "Silence," by Eugenio de Andrade
"Bon Voyage" – "Departure," by Pierre Reverdy

In addition to "free-flight," four other poems in this book came about as direct responses to poems by the extraordinary Québec poet José Aquelin, translated by Antonio D'Alfonso in *The Man Who Delivers Clouds* (Guernica Editions, 2011). They are: "Valuation," "Nocturne," "Quasi-Dedalian," and "Advice."

I thank all of the members of the following poetry groups and workshops for the constructive feedback many of my poems-in-progress received over the past few years: the Vic poets; the Vaughan Poets' Circle, led by Debbie Ouellet; the TOPS group organized by Bunny Iskov; the Literary Lobsters; and the Toronto Renaissance Conspiracy, led by Diane Mascherin.

I am especially grateful to John Reibetanz, Richard Greene, David Zieroth, and Bruce Hunter for their astute comments on early versions of my manuscript.

## OTHER QUATTRO POETRY BOOKS